FALKIRK COMMUNITY TRUST

30124 03088273 4

WBANK LIBRARY

D1389326

FALKIRK COMMUNITY
TRUST LIBRARIES

Women in
Science

By Jen Green

Editor Kritika Gupta
Senior Art Editor Ann Cannings
Art Editor Roohi Rais
Jacket Co-ordinator Francesca Young
Jacket Designers Amy Keast, Suzena Sengupta
Illustrator Mohd Zishan
DTP Designers Dheeraj Singh, Vikram Singh
Senior Picture Researcher Sumedha Chopra
Producer, Pre-Production Rob Dunn
Producer Niamh Tierney
Managing Editors Deborah Lock, Monica Saigal
Managing Art Editor Diane Peyton Jones
Deputy Managing Art Editor Ivy Sengupta
Art Director Martin Wilson
Publisher Sarah Larter
Publishing Director Sophie Mitchell

Reading Consultant Jacqueline Harris
Subject Consultant Elizabeth Maurer
National Women's History Museum

First published in Great Britain in 2018
by Dorling Kinderslely Limited
80 Strand, London, WC2R 0RL

Copyright © 2018 Dorling Kindersley Limited
A Penguin Random House Company
18 19 20 21 22 10 9 8 7 6 5 4 3 2 1
001—307849—Feb/18

All rights reserved.
No part of this publication may be reproduced, stored in or introduced into a retrieval system,
or transmitted, in any form, or by any means (electronic, mechanical, photocopying, recording,
or otherwise), without the prior written permission of the copyright owner.

A CIP catalogue record for this book is available from the British Library.
ISBN: 978-0-2413-1595-8

Printed and bound in China.

The publisher would like to thank the following for their kind permission to reproduce their photographs:

1 NASA: (b). 3 Dreamstime.com: Dmit Co. KG (tl); Photo Researchers / Scien Press Ltd. 11 Getty Images: Dea / Ver (bl). 14 Alamy Stock Photo: Pictorial Congress, Washington, D.C.: J.E. Pur Eric Feferberg (bl). Rex Shutterstock: Everett Collection Inc (tr). 22 Getty Shutterstock. 26 Dorling Kindersley Research Center (t). 30 Alamy Stock Images: Science & Society Picture Researchers / Science History Imag Images: Boston Globe. 38-39 Univer Stock Photo: Pictorial Press Ltd (l 43 Alamy Stock Photo: Kay & Karl An 44 Dorling Kindersley: The Science Mu bild (b). 47 Dorling Kindersley: RGB R (br). 50 Getty Images: Universal H Dreamstime.com: Johan Mollerberg Historical (tl). Getty Images: Pascal

tock Photo: bilwissedition Ltd. &). 8 Alamy Stock Photo: Pictorial rchers / Science History Images l History Archive (cl). Library of es (tl). Getty Images: Afp Photo / lves., (b). 21 Alamy Stock Photo: tock: United Artists / Kobal / !8 NASA: (b). 29 NASA: Langley ald Archive / SSPL (br). 31 Getty 33 Alamy Stock Photo: Photo :tion, UBC 1.1 / 11783. 37 Getty 1 Juliana Rotich: (br). 42 Alamy Vegative Number 155545 (cl). ubilet / National Geographic (tr). Images. 46 Getty Images: ullstei Jreamstime.com: Shawn Hempel Historical Picture Archive (cr). r Stock Photo: Everett Collection 3 University of Washington: (br)

Jacke
Endp

Falkirk Community Trust

30124 03088273 4

Askews & Holts	
J428.6	£4.99
MK	

For further information see: www.dkimages.com

A WORLD OF IDEAS:
SEE ALL THERE IS TO KNOW
www.dk.com

Contents

Scientists of ancient times

Since ancient times, women have had an important place in science. The names of many of these women are lost, but here are some we know about.

Merit Ptah

Merit Ptah is the first woman scientist we have a record of. She lived in Ancient Egypt 4,700 years ago. She was chief physician (doctor) at the pharaoh's court.

> **About 2700 BCE**

> **About 1200 BCE**

Tapputi

Tapputi was a chemist in Ancient Babylon (now Iraq). She worked as a perfume-maker in the royal palace. She invented a machine called a still for purifying alcohol.

Tapputi's tablet

Artemisia II of Caria

Artemisia II was queen of Caria (now in western Turkey). She was skilled at using herbs in medicine. The group of plants called Artemisia is named after her.

Metrodora

Metrodora worked as a physician in Ancient Greece. She wrote a book called *On the Diseases and Cures of Women*. It is the oldest medical book by a woman that has survived.

| 4ᵗʰ century BCE | 4ᵗʰ century CE | 5ᵗʰ century CE |

Hypatia

Hypatia was a Greek mathematician, astronomer and philosopher. She lived in Alexandria, Egypt, which was a great centre of learning. People came from many different countries to hear her teaching.

5

Chapter 1
Explorers of science

People have always asked questions about the world we live in. In past times, women made discoveries in mathematics, physics, chemistry and astronomy.

Women found out about stars, devised the first computer program and improved healthcare. They explored new fields, such as space engineering.

Telescope

For centuries, the work of women scientists was often hidden. Women were expected to stay at home and not to become scientists. Some women published using a male

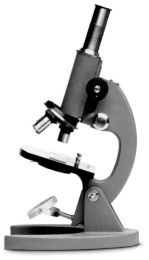

Microscope

name. Others weren't given money for research, or a proper place to work in. Lise Meitner and Marie Curie had to work in dark, dusty basements. Women's achievements have often been ignored, while male co-workers received praise.

The success of male and female scientists should always be celebrated. This book tells the stories of just a handful of great women from the world of science.

Test tube and flasks

Émilie du Châtelet's work was respected during her life.

Émilie du Châtelet (1706–1749) was a French noblewoman with a passion for science. Her partner, the French philosopher Voltaire, shared her interest. Châtelet set up a laboratory in her house where they both did experiments. In 1737, she wrote a paper on light and heat. It was the first paper by a woman to be published by the French Academy of Sciences.

Châtelet translated the English mathematician Isaac Newton's book, *Principia Mathematica*, into French. Newton's great work explored light, gravity and astronomy. Châtelet explained difficult sections and added her own experiments, which proved Newton's ideas. Her work helped to develop scientific knowledge and understanding at that time.

Maria Agnesi (1718–1799) was the eldest daughter of an Italian silk textile merchant. Agnesi was taught languages, maths and science by many private tutors. Her father made her give speeches on science to visitors to raise their importance in noble society. When she was 20, Agnesi published a collection of her speeches.

She believed in the importance of education for everyone. She wrote a maths textbook that was more than 1,000 pages long. It took her 10 years to write. At the age of 32, she was given an honorary diploma by Bologna University in Italy. She was the first woman to be given this honour.

This is a portrait of Maria Agnesi in around 1750.

D.M.GAETANA AGNESI

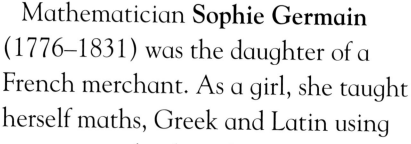

Mathematician **Sophie Germain** (1776–1831) was the daughter of a French merchant. As a girl, she taught herself maths, Greek and Latin using books in her father's library. In the 18th century, women could not study at colleges or universities. Germain wrote to professors in Paris asking for lecture notes.

Sophie Germain aged 14 years.

She signed herself "M. LeBlanc", the name of a male student she knew.

Germain became interested in the movements created by vibrations. She sent a paper about this to the French Academy of Sciences. On her third try, she won the Science Prize. Her work forms part of the mathematics that is used to build skyscrapers today.

Sand on a flat glass plate forms patterns when the plate is vibrated with a bow.

Mary Anning (1799–1847) came from a poor family. She grew up on England's south coast, where the cliffs contain fossils. As a young girl, she began collecting fossils to sell to wealthy visitors.

Mary Anning became one of the most famous fossil hunters.

This ichthyosaur fossil shows it had a tail, a fin and front paddles.

Fossil collecting was dangerous because the cliffs were steep and crumbly.

Around the age of 11, Anning spotted the skeleton of a dolphin-like sea reptile we now call an ichthyosaur. This was the first of many discoveries.

At the time, no one understood what fossils were. Anning's finds helped scientists realise that fossils were the remains of long-dead creatures that had slowly turned to stone. She greatly added to what we know about prehistoric life.

Ada Lovelace (1815–1852) was the daughter of the English poet Lord Byron. She showed an early talent for languages and mathematics. At the age of 17, she met a mathematician named Charles Babbage. He had invented a calculating machine called the Analytical Engine. Lovelace was inspired by his idea. She translated a French paper about the Engine into English, adding her own comments.

Lovelace began working with Charles. She worked out a way of using punched cards to input data into the Engine. Lovelace had invented the world's first computer program. She predicted that machines might be used to do all sorts of things, such as writing music. In this way, she imagined a future when computers would be used.

Punched cards

In 1838, Lady Ada King became Countess of Lovelace.

Heroes of healthcare

Women have contributed greatly to the fields of science and medicine over the years. They have made important discoveries in healthcare.

Florence Nightingale (1820–1910)
Nightingale was also known as the Lady with the Lamp. She was a British nurse who saved many soldiers during the Crimean War (1853–1856). She also improved the cleanliness of the army hospitals. This led to fewer deaths due to infection.

Clara Barton (1821–1912)
Barton collected and gave out medical supplies during the Civil War (1861–1865). She is widely known as the founder of the American Red Cross. Barton risked her life many times to save injured soldiers.

Mary Edwards Walker (1832–1919)

Walker was an American doctor. She was on field duty during the Civil War. Walker was the only woman surgeon at that time. She was awarded the Medal of Honor for her service during the war.

Jane Cooke Wright (1919–2013)

Wright came from a family of doctors working in cancer research. She developed new drugs and techniques for treating cancer. Her work saved many thousands of lives. She became the first female president of the New York Cancer Society.

Françoise Barré-Sinoussi (1947–)

Barré-Sinoussi is a French scientist. She discovered the HIV virus. Her research in this area has helped to improve the treatment for the disease. In 2008, Barré-Sinoussi won the Nobel Prize in medicine.

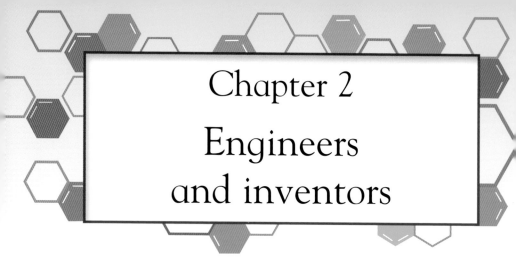

Chapter 2
Engineers and inventors

Brooklyn Bridge in New York is one of America's most famous landmarks. But did you know that a woman was in charge of its completion?

Brooklyn Bridge

Emily Roebling
(1843–1903) was the
wife of civil engineer
Washington Roebling.
Washington's father,
John Roebling, designed
the Brooklyn Bridge.
When he died,
Washington managed
its construction. Emily
studied engineering,
so she could help
her husband.

Emily was the first person
to cross the Brooklyn
Bridge in May 1881.

In 1872, Washington became seriously
ill. Emily took over managing the building
of the bridge, communicating with
politicians, engineers and builders in
the process. This continued for 14 years,
until the bridge was finished. A plaque
on the bridge honours the work of Emily,
Washington and John Roebling.

Beulah Henry (1887–1973) was an American inventor. She registered 49 patents. This is a government licence that gives you the sole right to make and sell your invention.

Beulah Henry attending the Exposition of Women's Arts and Industries event in New York, 1931.

Many of Henry's inventions were designed to use at work or at home. She developed her first invention while still at college. It was an ice cream freezer.

Old ice cream freezer

Henry also invented an umbrella. She founded a company to make and sell the umbrella in New York. Later she improved the workings of a sewing machine, typewriters and a machine to make paper copies. The money she made from her inventions was enough to live on. This was unusual for a woman at that time, as most women didn't earn their own money.

Hedy Lamarr (1914–2000) was a movie actress. Few people knew she was also an inventor. She helped develop technology that is used in mobile communications today. Lamarr was born in Austria. She moved to America and became a screen actress, but her secret passion was inventing.

During World War II, Lamarr had an idea for improving radio-guided torpedoes. These missiles regularly missed their targets when the enemy jammed the signal. Lamarr teamed up with a composer named George Antheil. The pair worked out a way of coding the signals by varying the radio frequencies used. The idea was developed in the 1960s and is used in Wi-Fi and mobile phones today.

Lamarr wasn't recognised for her idea until the 1970s. This photo is a film still.

The 1950s and 1960s were an exciting time for space exploration. The United States and the Soviet Union (now Russia) raced to develop the technology to explore space. The Americans promised to land humans on the moon. This rivalry between the two great powers is called the Space Race.

Three African-American women, Katherine Johnson, Dorothy Vaughan and Mary Jackson, played a vital role in the American space programme.

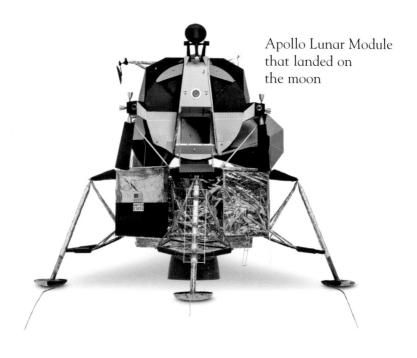

Apollo Lunar Module that landed on the moon

Dorothy Vaughan (*left*) celebrates with her colleagues Leslie Hunter (*centre*) and Vivian Adair (*right*) from NASA.

They and other women, such as Leslie Hunter and Vivian Adair, worked for the American space agency, NASA. They were all brilliant mathematicians. In the days before digital computers, they were known as human computers. They worked out the flight paths of spacecraft orbiting the Earth and later travelling to the moon.

Katherine Johnson (1918–) worked out the flight paths of early manned space missions called the Mercury programme. Later she calculated the course of the Apollo spacecraft that made the first moon landing. She also worked on space shuttle missions.

Katherine Johnson working at NASA Langley Research Centre, in 1966.

Mary Jackson became an engineer at NASA Langley Research Centre.

Mary Jackson (1921–2005) worked as a computer programmer, and then as an engineer. She became the first black female engineer. She is an inspiration to female scientists and engineers.

Dorothy Vaughan (1910–2008) was a supervisor at NASA. When the space agency switched to digital computers, Vaughan taught herself computer programming. Then she trained her fellow workers.

Reach for the stars

Women have been studying space for centuries. Today, women work as astronauts and are involved in every branch of space science.

Cecilia Payne-Gaposchkin (1900–1979)

Payne-Gaposchkin was a British-American astronomer. She was the first to claim that the Sun is made of hydrogen and helium gas. Other experts didn't believe her, but Payne-Gaposchkin was right. She later became a professor of astronomy.

Jocelyn Bell Burnell (1943–)

Burnell is an astrophysicist from Northern Ireland. As a research student, she helped build a giant radio telescope. She discovered radio waves pulsing from deep space. The team worked out these were coming from small, dense stars we now call pulsars.

Sally Ride (1951–2012)

Ride was an American physicist and astronaut. In 1983, at age 32, she became the first American female astronaut. She flew two space shuttle missions, and then became a professor of physics at the University of California.

Mae Jemison (1956–)

Jemison is an American engineer, doctor and astronaut. After medical school, she worked for the Peace Corps in Africa. In 1992, she became the first African-American in space aboard the Space Shuttle *Endeavour*.

Maggie Aderin-Pocock (1968–)

Aderin-Pocock is a British space scientist and has built instruments for the European Space Agency and NASA satellites and systems. She is also a science presenter for television.

Chapter 3
Computer scientists

Computer scientists develop ways to use new technology. They design software, and they use computers to solve problems.

Grace Hopper (1906–1992) was a mathematician and computer programmer. She was also a high-ranking officer in the US Navy. During World War II, she left her job as a college professor to join the Navy. The military sent her to Harvard University to programme an electronic computer, called the Harvard Mark I.

When the war ended, she left the Navy to work for a private business. She headed the team that invented COBOL, the first user-friendly computer language.

This language allowed people to "talk" to computers. At the age of 60, she returned to the Navy. She served for another 19 years and became a rear admiral, before finally retiring at the age of 79.

The Harvard Mark I was huge at 16 metres (51 feet) long!

Charlotte Fischer was a professor at the University of British Columbia, Canada from 1957 to 1968.

Charlotte Fischer (1929–) is a Canadian physicist, building computer programs to help with difficult calculations. She was born in present-day Ukraine, but soon after went to Canada with her family. She studied first as a mathematician and chemist, but her interest in solving equations led her to calculating the structure of atoms.

Fischer combined physics with computer science to create a groundbreaking computer program. Her equations are so complicated, only modern computers are powerful enough to solve them. She is a college professor and has published more than 250 scientific papers.

Shafrira Goldwasser (1958–) is an American-Israeli computer scientist. She was born in New York to Israeli parents. The family moved to Israel when she was a girl. At school, she did well in physics, maths and literature.

Goldwasser went back to the USA to continue her studies. There she became interested in computer programming and especially cryptography. This is the process of coding information on the Internet so it stays private, and cannot be read by just anyone. She co-invented zero-knowledge proofs, which are a key tool in protecting coded data. She holds the post of professor at two universities, in the USA and Israel.

Shafrira Goldwasser won an award for her work in cryptography in 2012.

Yoky Matsuoka (1972–) is an expert in robotics – the design and use of robots. She grew up in Japan. There she played tennis at a high level, until an injury forced her to give it up. At the age of 16, she moved to the USA to study computer science and engineering. She became interested in how robotics could help people with disabilities.

Matsuoka has developed technology to help people with movement problems. For example, she developed a robotic arm that the user moves using virtual reality technology. She has also worked on the technology for smart homes. This allows homeowners to adjust heating and other systems in their homes via the Internet.

Yoky Matsuoka holds a robotic arm with fingers that have a range of movement.

Massachusetts Institute of Technology, USA

Radia Perlman (1951–) is a computer engineer and software designer. In the 1970s, she studied mathematics at the Massachusetts Institute of Technology, USA. There were very few other women students in her classes.

In 1985, she designed the Spanning Tree Protocol (STP). This program allows computer networks to link safely, and helps make the Internet possible. Perlman has been called "the mother of the Internet", and won many awards.

Juliana Rotich (1977–) is an expert in information technology. She was born in Kenya. She studied information technology in the USA before returning to Kenya. Rotich co-founded the software company Ushahidi. This company develops free software to improve Internet access for Africa and the developing world.

Juliana Rotich supports young people interested in technology.

Natural scientists

Women have made many discoveries about plants, nature and animals. Here are a few of the most famous scientists in this field.

Florence Hawley Ellis (1906–1991)

Anthropologists study human societies, past or present. Ellis studied Native American cultures of the southwestern USA. She was one of the first scientists to use tree rings in tree trunks to record the age of trees and date objects.

Rachel Carson (1907–1964)

Conservationists work to protect nature. Carson was a pioneer of conservation. Her book *Silent Spring* showed that a plant spray called DDT was killing wildlife. DDT is now banned in most countries.

Eugenie Clark
(1922–2015)

Marine biologist Clark was known as "the Shark Lady". She was one of the first scientists to study sharks and tropical fish underwater, using scuba-diving gear.

Dian Fossey
(1932–1985)

Zoologist Fossey studied gorillas in Central Africa. Her book, *Gorillas in the Mist*, was made into a film. Fossey's work helped people understand and protect these gentle animals.

Jane Goodall
(1934–)

Goodall is a primatologist – an expert in chimpanzee behaviour. She discovered that chimps used tools, such as stones to open nuts. Her work helped people understand that chimps and humans are closely related.

Chapter 4
Super scientists

Certain scientists have been celebrated for their achievements. They have received prizes and awards.

Marie Curie (1867–1934) was a Polish scientist. She is best known for her research into fighting cancer. In 1891, Curie moved to Paris, France, to study. She investigated the invisible rays given off by an element called uranium. She called these rays "radioactivity". Curie worked with her husband, Pierre Curie.

Glass flask used by Marie Curie for experiments

They discovered two chemical elements. These were named polonium and radium. Curie won the Nobel Prize for Physics in 1903. She was the first woman to win a Nobel Prize.

She continued to work on the medical uses of radioactivity. In 1911, she won the Nobel Prize for Chemistry. She is the only person who has won two Nobel Prizes in different sciences.

Marie Curie working in her laboratory.

Chemist **Lise Meitner** (1878–1968) was born in Vienna, Austria, to Jewish parents. In 1907, she went to Berlin in Germany and met fellow researcher Otto Hahn at the university. They studied the chemical element uranium.

Jews and women were banned from the university buildings, so Meitner had to work in a dark basement.

Uranium

In the 1930s, the anti-Jewish Nazi Party came to power in Germany. Meitner escaped to Sweden but continued working with Hahn. The pair discovered that splitting uranium released vast amounts of energy. Meitner called this process nuclear fission. In 1944, Hahn received a Nobel Prize for their discovery, but Meitner was not honoured. The element meitnerium is named after her.

Lise Meitner (*right*) working with her colleague Berta Karlik (*left*) in 1953.

X-ray crystallography is the study of crystals using X-rays. British scientist **Dorothy Hodgkin** (1910–1994) was a pioneer in this technique, which is used to show the structure of molecules.

Dorothy Hodgkin experimenting in her laboratory in 1964.

Hodgkin studied chemistry at Oxford University, UK. She spent years working out the structure of insulin. This vital hormone is used to manage the disease diabetes. Next she discovered the structure of the antibiotic penicillin. Antibiotics are medicines used to treat bacterial infection. Her work allowed scientists to make large amounts of penicillin, which saved many thousands of lives.

Hodgkin went on to map the structure of vitamin B12. In 1964, she won a Nobel Prize in Chemistry. She also worked to promote world peace.

Structure of vitamin B12

DNA is the molecule inside cells that controls the genes inherited from parents. **Rosalind Franklin** (1920–1958) was a British scientist who made a breakthrough in understanding DNA.

Franklin researched DNA in the 1950s. The structure and workings of DNA were a mystery at the time.

Rosalind Franklin produced the first clear images of DNA molecules.

Franklin took an X-ray photo of the molecule. Another researcher, Maurice Wilkins, showed it to two scientists, Francis Crick and James Watson. The photo showed that DNA has a structure like a twisted ladder. This structure unzips to make new molecules, allowing features to pass from parents to children.

Franklin died in 1958. Four years later, Crick, Watson and Wilkins won a Nobel Prize for the discovery of DNA's structure. Franklin's work was only honoured in this century.

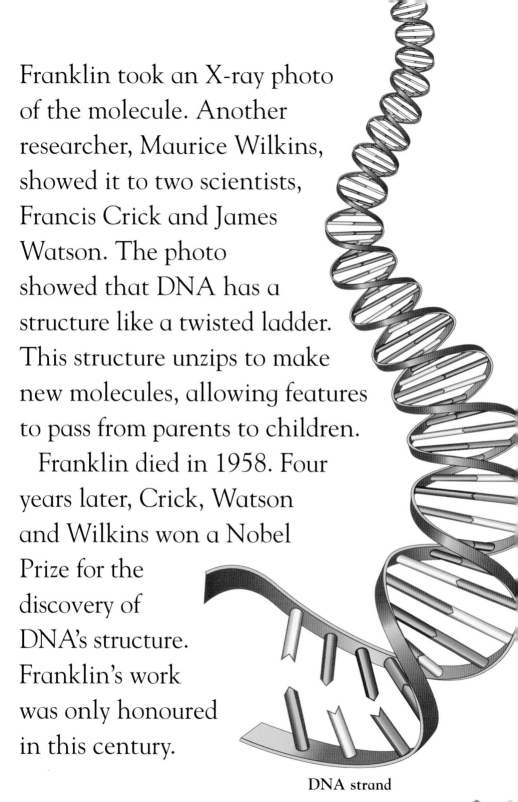

DNA strand

Chien-Shiung Wu (1912–1997) was a Chinese-American nuclear physicist. She grew up in China, and then went to the USA to study physics. Her research involved splitting uranium atoms to make radioactive elements called isotopes. These are used in a range of things from medical treatments to smoke detectors. After graduating, she became a professor.

During World War II, she worked on the top-secret Manhattan Project. The aim was to develop the first atomic bomb. Wu developed the bomb's fuel and a radiation detector. Atomic bombs dropped on Japan in 1945 led to the end of World War II. Wu then did research into how radioactive elements decay, releasing energy over time. She has inspired many girls to become scientists.

Chien-Shiung Wu
researching at Columbia
University, USA.

Nobel Prize winners

Nobel Prizes are given to people who make progress in science and culture. Here are some of the many female scientists who have received the award.

Nobel Prize medal

Gerty Cori
(1896–1957)

Gerty and her husband, Carl Cori, were Czech chemists. They moved to the USA to carry out research. They discovered how our cells use sugar for energy. This process is called the Cori cycle. They won a Nobel Prize in 1947.

Irène Joliot-Curie
(1897–1956)

Irène was the daughter of scientists Marie and Pierre Curie. With her husband, Frédéric Joliot, she discovered how to make radioactive elements artificially. This French couple won a Nobel Prize in 1935.

Barbara McClintock
(1902–1992)

McClintock did pioneering work in genetics. This is the study of genes, the tiny units that determine inherited traits. McClintock studied maize genes. She discovered that genes could change in response to the environment. She won a Nobel Prize in 1983.

Gertrude Elion
(1918–1999)

Elion was an American biochemist, who did research into cancer. She helped develop medicines to treat cancer and viruses such as HIV. Her work has saved thousands of lives. She shared a Nobel Prize in 1988.

May-Britt Moser
(1963–)

This Norwegian scientist researches how the brain works and how we form memories. With her husband, Edvard, she discovered a new type of cell, called grid cells. These are vital to memory and help us find our way in new places. The Mosers won a Nobel Prize in 2014.

Careers in science

There are many different fields of science. In each field, there are exciting areas to research and new discoveries to be made.

Engineering and space technology to study engineering, construction and aerospace.

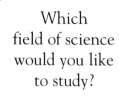

Which field of science would you like to study?

Information technology to study computer science, IT, robotics and artificial intelligence (AI).

Genetics to explore the secrets of heredity and pioneer new techniques in genetics.

Biology and Earth science to explore the variety of life on Earth, and make new discoveries about how the planet works.

Energy to build new technologies for energy without causing pollution.

Agriculture and environmental research to provide food for growing human populations and protect habitats and wildlife worldwide.

Medicine to find cures for viruses, cancer and other diseases.

Who will be the next scientist to make a great breakthrough? It could be you.

Quiz

1 Name the oldest medical book written by a woman.

2 What was the male name used by Sophie Germain to write to professors at universities?

3 Who invented the world's first computer program?

4 What was Florence Nightingale known as?

5 What was Beulah Henry's first invention?

6 Who was the first American female astronaut?

7 Who programmed the electronic computer Harvard Mark I?

8 Who is known as "the mother of the Internet"?

9 Who wrote the book *Gorillas in the Mist*?

10 Which element is named after Lise Meitner?

11 Who produced the first clear images of DNA molecules?

12 When did Barbara McClintock win the Nobel Prize?

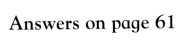

Answers on page 61

Glossary

access
entry to a place, organisation or the Internet

anthropologist
scientist who studies cultures, society and people

astrophysicist
scientist who studies stars, planets and other objects
in space

conservationist
person who works to protect the natural world
and wildlife

cryptography
art of writing or solving codes, for example to keep
data secure (private) on the Internet

data
information

electronic
devices that operate using parts that control
and direct electricity

frequency
rate per second of a wave, such as a radio wave

genetics
study of heredity and genes, the units of inheritance

hormone
chemical substance in the body that controls how
certain cells and organs work

information technology
study and use of systems such as computers and phones
to store and send information

molecule
smallest unit of a substance that has all the properties
of that substance

nuclear fission
when the nucleus of an atom splits, releasing energy

patent
government licence giving inventors the sole right
to sell and make their inventions

pulsar
small, dense star that rotates, giving off pulses of radio waves

radioactive
produces energy from the breaking up of atoms

robotics
design and use of robots

software
programs and other operating systems used by computers

virus
tiny living thing that causes infection

Wi-Fi
system that allows devices such as computers and
smartphones to connect to the Internet without wires

zoologist
scientist who studies animals and their behaviour

Answers to the Quiz:

1. *On the Diseases and Cures of Women*; 2. M. le Blanc;
3. Ada Lovelace; 4. Lady with the lamp; 5. Ice cream freezer;
6. Sally Ride; 7. Grace Hopper; 8. Radia Perlman; 9. Dian
Fossey; 10. Meitnerium; 11. Rosalind Franklin; 12. 1983

Index

Yoky Matsuoka holds a robotic arm

A LEVEL FOR EVERY READER

This book is a part of an exciting four-level reading series to support children in developing the habit of reading widely for both pleasure and information. Each book is designed to develop a child's reading skills, fluency, grammar awareness and comprehension in order to build confidence and enjoyment when reading.

> **Ready for a Level 3 (Beginning to Read Alone) book**
>
> A child should:
>
> - be able to read many words without needing to stop and break them down into sound parts.
> - read smoothly, in phrases and with expression, and at a good pace.
> - self-correct when a word or sentence doesn't sound right or doesn't make sense.

A valuable and shared reading experience

For many children, reading requires much effort but adult participation can make reading both fun and easier. Here are a few tips on how to use this book with a young reader:

Check out the contents together:

- read about the book on the back cover and talk about the contents page to help heighten interest and expectation.
- ask the reader to make predictions about what they think will happen next.
- talk about the information he/she might want to find out.

Encourage fluent reading:

- encourage reading aloud in fluent, expressive phrases, making full use of punctuation and thinking about the meaning; if helpful, choose a sentence to read aloud to help demonstrate reading with expression.

Praise, share and talk:

- notice if the reader is responding to the text by self-correcting and varying his/her voice.
- encourage the reader to recall specific details after each chapter.
- let her/him pick out interesting words and discuss what they mean.
- talk about what he/she found most interesting or important and show your own enthusiasm for the book.
- read the quiz at the end of the book and encourage the reader to answer the questions, if necessary, by turning back to the relevant pages to find the answers.